Valencia, Benidorm & the Costa Blanca Travel Guide

Attractions, Eating, Drinking, Shopping & Places To Stay

Sophie Bell

Copyright © 2014, Astute Press
All Rights Reserved.

No part of this publication may be reproduced, stored in a retrieval system, or transmitted, in any form or by any means without the prior written permission of the publisher, nor be otherwise circulated in any form of binding or cover other than that in which it is published and without similar condition being imposed on the subsequent purchaser.

If there are any errors or omissions in copyright acknowledgements the publisher will be pleased to insert the appropriate acknowledgement in any subsequent printing of this publication.

Although we have taken all reasonable care in researching this book we make no warranty about the accuracy or completeness of its content and disclaim all liability arising from its use

Table of Contents

Valencia 7
Planning Your Stay 14
Climate & Weather 16
Sightseeing 19
   Cabacera Park & Valencia Bio Parc 19
   Cathedral 21
   Silk Market (La Lonja de Seda) 22
   Central Market 24
   Serranos Towers 25
   City of Arts & Sciences 26
   Hemisfèric Cinema 27
   Science Museum Príncipe Felipe 27
   Oceanogràfic Aquarium 28
   Palau de les Arts 29
   Umbracle (City of Arts & Sciences) 30
   Ágora Events Arena 31
   Museum of Enlightenment & Modernity 32
   Monastery San Miguel de los Reyes 32
   Palacio del Marques de Dos Aguas & Museo Nacional de Cerámica González Martí 34
   Church of Saint John Hospital 35
   Almoina Archaeological Museum 36
Recommendations for the Budget Traveller 38
   Places to Stay 38
      Purple Nest Hostel 39
      Hotel Petit Germanias 39
      Petit Palace Bristol Hotel 40
      Medium Hotels 40
   Eating & Drinking 41
      Restaurante La Santa Compana 41
      Restaurante L'Estimat 41
      Lambrusqueria 42
      La Bodeguilla del Gato 43
      L'Umbracle Terraza 43

  Casa Montana..44
  Carmen Neighborhood 44
 Shopping **45**
  El Corte Ingles...46
  Calle La Pau & Calle Marques de Dos Aigue.....................47
  Valencia F.C. Shop at the Train Station 47
  Calle Don Juan de Austria & Calle Colon 48
  Teashop 48

Benidorm, Alicante & Costa Blanca 49
 Culture **51**
 Location & Orientation..**52**
 Climate & When to Visit **52**

Sightseeing Highlights..54
 Visit the Old City of Valencia **54**
 Casco Antiguo, Benidorm...**56**
 Island of Tabarca, Alicante **57**
 Catch the Sun at Playa de Poniente, Benidorm **59**
 The Castle of Santa Bárbara, Alicante **60**
 Aqualandia Water Park, Benidorm.......................................**61**
 Mundomar, Benidorm **62**
 Terra Mitica, Benidorm **63**
 Hiking in the Alicante Mountains **64**
 Terra Natura, Benidorm **66**
 Stroll the Explanada de España, Alicante............................**67**
 Eat Chocolate in Villajoyosa **67**
 Bask in the Shade of Palms of Elche.....................................**68**

Recommendations for the Budget Traveller 71
 Places to Stay...**71**
  Gran Hotel Bali, Benidorm 71
  Hotel Abaco Altea..72
  Servigroup Nereo, Benidorm 73
  Villa Del Mar Hotel, Benidorm...73
  Hospes Amerigo, Alicante 74
 Places to Eat & Drink **75**
  Déjà Vu, Benidorm..75
  Bocaito, Alicante..76
  Nou Manolin, Alicante 76
  Kataria Gastronomica, Benidorm...77
  El Chipiron Freiduria, Alicante...78
 Places to Shop..**78**

Plaza Mayor at Casco Antiguo, Benidorm..79
La Marina Shopping Center, Benidorm 79
Guitarras Cashmira, Gata de Gorgos 80
El Cisne Flea Market, Benidorm..80
Artesano de Polop, Benidorm..81

Valencia

The Spanish city of Valencia has a curious charm all its own. There are remnants of ancient history dating back to 138 B.C. rubbing shoulders with ultra-modern buildings that have sprung up since the America's Cup was held here twice in the last few years.

Valencia never used to be high on the list of tourist destinations but took a sudden leap to fame when the America's Cup was held here in 2007 and again in 2010. Vast sums of money were invested in massive redevelopment programmes especially around the docks and marina which were transformed into attractive and tourist-friendly places to visit.

To the north of the docks and marina, the wide, flat beaches stretch for miles lapped by the clear blue Mediterranean Sea. The soft golden sands of Las Arenas, Cabañal and Malvarrosa are great places for families to visit. There are all the facilities needed for a great day at the beach with play parks for the children, toilets, shops and plenty of places to eat and drink. Most of the beachside restaurants (chiringuitos) have a BBQ or open fire blazing outside and the smell of sardines cooking as you walk past can be very tempting. Accompanied by a plate of salad the sardines make a tasty meal washed down with a glass of local wine. The tree lined promenade running alongside the beach is just right for a gentle stroll after a meal or just to soak up the sights and sounds of people having a good time.

There is something for everyone here and the city attracts not just holidaymakers but business travellers as well. Valencia is now is one of the leading cities in Europe for conferences and business fairs with facilities that are the envy of many places. If you are looking for designer shopping a good starting point is Calle Colón and the nearby streets where there is every brand name you could wish for. Leaving Calle Colón go towards the Plaza del Ayuntamiento and on to Barrio del Carmen in the Old Town where the shops become more individual and Spanish.

The Romans founded the city and the Old Town area around the Barrio del Carmen with its twisty narrow streets is a good place to start to find reminders of these ancient times. There is some beautiful architecture here amongst the brightly painted houses. Remember to take your time and look up at the buildings, some of the most striking architecture is often above street level. Most of these streets are too narrow for vehicles so watch out for mopeds hurtling round the corners.

There are plenty of bars and restaurants in the daytime but when nighttime comes it is just amazing how many more appear as if from nowhere. Doorways open to reveal tiny tapas bars sometimes with only one or two tables inside. Elsewhere shutters go up and the distinctive sound of flamenco music can be heard drifting through the streets mixed with disco. The Barrio is a cosmopolitan mix of every nationality and ethnic origin. The bars and clubs reflect this with places to suit all tastes, however wide and varied they may be.

In Spain nobody goes out 'early'. No self-respecting Spaniard would go out until at least 10pm and that is only if they plan on eating before making the most of the night time entertainment. In the hot summer months by midnight the streets surrounding the Plaza del Ayuntamiento will be full of couples of all ages wandering hand in hand, families enjoying a stroll in the cooler night air or just groups of friends wanting to chat over a few drinks.

The city of Valencia has many ancient buildings and historical sites that have stood for many hundreds of years and part of their attraction is the impact of time. The city is also full of modern architecture and one of the most striking buildings in Valencia stands on the site of the riverbed. The Turia River used to run through the city but the farsighted city designers realised that there was a better use for all this space and turned it into a park that now houses the City of Arts and Sciences. Designed by Santiago Calatrava and Félix Candelaat, construction started in 1996 with the final part of the project completed in 2005. The complex comprises a Science Museum, an IMAX cinema, the biggest aquarium in Europe, a multi-purpose venue and conference centre, plus an art and culture centre. A vantage point called the Umbracle is simply beautiful and is an area for walks, relaxation and taking in the views over the whole complex. There are various exhibitions held in and around this area and it also contains the Garden of Astronomy where much can be learnt about the stars.

Visitors to Valencia might be surprised to see many signposts and street names in not just Spanish (Castilian) but also in the local language (Valencian). It is a good idea to be aware of this although the Valencianos are not quite as sensitive to the linguistic issue as the people of Barcelona who feel even more strongly in favour of their native language of Catalan. Most people in Valencia speak Spanish as their first language these days with only some of the older residents being completely fluent in Valencian. Some of the younger people will have learnt English at school but it is still not that common to find fluent English speaking locals. Most English is spoken around the marina where the cruise ships come in.

Valencia is famous for being the birthplace of the well-known and much-loved Spanish dish called Paella. The Moors introduced the growing of rice to the area over a millennium ago and now several varieties are cultivated in the rice growing area of La Albufera. The growing of rice involves a year round painstaking process for the rice farmers who lovingly prepare the fields and then tend to their crops so we can benefit from these simple white grains. In April the 3000 hectare Albufera lagoon along with the river Jucar floods over 14000 hectares of land which produces some 120 million kilos of rice every year.

As in many Spanish towns, many festivals are held during the year in and around Valencia. The one not to be missed is in March and is called Las Fallas and it features the most spectacular display of fire, music, dancing, pyrotechnics, fireworks and noise you will probably ever witness! Estimates as to how many visitors flock to see this deafening spectacle every year varies somewhere between two and three million people. The earth-shattering noise of the strings of mascleta firecrackers at 2pm each day of the festival can be heard and seen up close in the Plaza del Ayuntamiento and just about everywhere else as the whole city reverberates with the cannon-like explosions. The level of noise is such that pregnant women are actually discouraged from attending.

The Fallas themselves are huge sculptures made from wood and papier-mâché standing about 15 metres tall. These effigies can take the whole year to make and the current trend is to base them on celebrities and politicians. The festival starts on the 12th March and the Fallas are placed in the streets overnight on the 15th and 16th March. Leading up to the Fallas being displayed there are many bullfights, pageants, parades, competitions and much more to see and take part in.

Visitors can walk the city admiring each Falla while taking advantage of the many stalls serving food and drink and while listening to the music in a party-like atmosphere. On the stroke of midnight on the 19th March the Fallas go up in flames with more explosions being provided by fireworks hidden inside each one and then it is over for another year.

Huge paellas are cooked in the streets to feed the hungry crowds at Las Fallas by specialist companies in pans that can be up to several metres across. According to the Guinness Book of Records the largest Paella in the world was cooked by a Valencian in 1992 in a pan that measured 65 feet in diameter. It fed 110,000 people.

It would be wrong to not mention football when talking about Valencia. The successful Valencia C.F. team has a very strong following and has been the winner of the Spanish League and the UEFA Cup as well as UEFA Champions League runner up. The home stadium of Valencia C.F. is the Mestella where 55,000 fans can watch the beautiful game.

For a shopping experience visit one of the many markets. The Central Market is the place to go for fresh produce; the stalls are piled high with colourful and sometimes unusual foods while the vendors shout out what often sounds like unintelligible gibberish. Many of the stalls will have sample plates of their products to tempt you, so don't be shy and have a taste of fruit, cheese, fish, meat, ham, wines and sherries or whatever they might be offering. Even if you don't want to buy anything this market has to be visited just to admire the fantastic building it is housed in. From the outside it is quite hard to believe that anything as humble as a market could be inside such splendour. The arched windows and magnificent stonework are topped off by a spectacular dome which lets the light flood in to illuminate the 300 market stalls. It is not to be missed.

To visit a good car boot sale, head to El Rastro. You will definitely find some treasures amongst all the sometimes useless items, and if not it is also a good place to pick up some genuine souvenirs.

The Ruzafa market on Mondays is the place to go for cheap and cheerful clothes, toys, games, linen and other general market stuff. There is plenty to choose from, the quality might not be great but if you want something bright and colourful to wear to the beach it is a good place to go.

Planning Your Stay

Valencia is located on the Costa del Azahar on Spain's Mediterranean coast which covers the 80 miles from Catalonia in the north to the Costa Blanca in the south. The self-governing region of Valencia is divided into three provinces, Alicante, Castellon and Valencia itself. Just below the halfway point on this stretch of coast, at the mouth of the Turia river (on the Gulf of Valencia) is the magnificent city of Valencia.

The Costa del Azahar is Spain's Orange Blossom Coast and a visit to the region in springtime makes it easy to see why. Orange groves full of trees with shiny green leaves and creamy white blossom stretch as far as the eye can see in this fertile land. By autumn the trees are dotted with bright orange as the fruits ripen ready to be picked. The fragrant scent of orange blossom is everywhere and it is a perfume that you will never forget.

In terms of population, Valencia is the third largest city in Spain with just over 800,000 inhabitants in the city and another million in the surrounding area. Valencia is equidistant from the other major cities of Barcelona and Madrid (both about 220 miles away) and Valencia is easily accessible by road and rail from both.

Valencia has two railway stations which are only ten minutes walk apart. Daily connections are available by rail from the Norte station in the heart of the city across not only Spain but also to Port Bou on the French/Spanish border. The newer Joaquim Sorolla station is used by the high speed and long distance trains to Madrid, Barcelona and Alicante. The AVE train to Madrid travels at 200 miles per hour.

The train service between Valencia Norte station and Valencia Airport runs from Monday to Friday every 30 minutes and the daily Aero-Bus service runs between the city and the airport every twenty minutes. Valencia (Manises) Airport lies to the west of the city and is the second busiest airport in the region after Alicante and the eighth busiest in the country. Flights from Valencia are available to many European airports as well as to North Africa and the Canary Islands.

Road connections to all of Spain are extensive with the AP-7 motorway running close to Valencia. The motorway runs the length of Spain and makes travelling from north to south easy and it provides a straight-through connection to France and the rest of Europe. Madrid is easily accessible via the A-3.

For sauntering around the flat streets of Valencia there is a public bicycle rental service called Valenbisi. There are 250 bicycle stations around the city and tickets can be purchased at any of these on a daily or weekly basis.

The Port of Valencia is the largest port in Spain and the fifth busiest seaport in Europe. Due to its central location on the Mediterranean coast it is the second busiest container port in Spain and handles around 60 million tonnes of cargo a year. For many years it was a dull and unattractive industrial area, with hundreds of containers stacked up against a skyline of cranes and winches with not much else to recommend it. The only visitors to the area apart from the dock workers used to be travellers wishing to board the ferries to the Balearic Islands.

When Valencia was chosen by Switzerland to host the 2007 America's Cup a massive transformation of the dock area and the old marina began. The Juan Carlos 1 Marina was renovated and is now home to trendy bars and restaurants. The marina is to the east of the city next to the Las Arenas and Malvarrosa beaches. Cruise ships call in bringing passengers from all around the world eager to sample the delights that the centre of Valencia and the surrounding areas have to offer.

Climate & Weather

Valencia has a great climate of long, warm to hot summers and mild winters. It has a sub-tropical climate and the summer season runs from April through until November.

The summer season is best for sunbathing when the daytime high can hit 34°C in August which is pleasant but not as meltingly hot as some of the more southern areas of Spain. The evenings are balmy and drop down to around 22°C which is ideal for dining al fresco at one of the many wonderful restaurants followed by a stroll along the promenade.

For a winter holiday January will be the coldest month, although that rather depends on your idea of cold. In the daytime the mercury hovers at 14°C but at night a chill sets in and the temperature can very quickly dip down sometimes as low as 2°C.

Spanish homes are not often equipped for cooler nights so warm night clothes are a good idea and tiled floors can be freezing to bare feet so socks or slippers are a must. Valencia is actually on the same latitude as Madrid yet the climates are very different. The temperature can drop well below freezing at night with sharp frosts and there are several ski areas just to the north of Madrid.

For sightseeing or a just a pleasant city break spring and autumn offer the best of everything. The temperature is mild, although it can rain, sometimes torrentially. Rain storms in the main are short and very heavy with water cascading down the street one minute and gone the next. Another advantage to not going in high season is that everywhere is generally less crowded, but if you choose the middle of March to visit watch out for the hoards that flock to Valencia for the Las Fallas festival. The spring months have an average high of 18°C with a low of 7°C, while the autumn figures are 23°C and 13°C. While this might feel warm to some people you can be sure the locals will still be wearing many layers of clothes.

The lucky Valencianos get more than their fair share of vitamin D each year as the yearly sunshine figures are 2,660, a whopping 70% more than the northern half of Europe. There is also more daylight with up to ten hours per day in the winter months with London or Moscow only getting around eight.

Sightseeing

Cabacera Park & Valencia Bio Parc

Avenida Pío Baroja, 3
46015 Valencia
Tel: +34 902 250 340
www.bioparcvalencia.es

In 2008 the Bioparc opened its doors to the public on the old Turia riverbed in the centre of Valencia.

Covering 25 acres within the Cabacera Park this innovative zoo has no apparent barriers so visitors feel like they are really out in the wild with the animals.

In their native Africa, right across the Savannah to Madagascar and Equatorial Africa, flora and fauna of many species co-exist and this has been recreated in Valencia. Elephants, leopards, hyenas, giraffes, hippopotamuses, lions, lemurs and ostriches are just a few of the species that live peacefully here side by side.

There are two snack bars within the Bioparc as well as a restaurant that serves a reasonably priced daily menu. Souvenirs and traditional African handicrafts can be purchased in the well-stocked gift shop. The Valencia BioParc is open every day of the year from 10am with the earliest closing being 6pm in the winter and slightly later in the summer. Admission prices are €24 per adult and €18 for children. There are concessions for students, groups and large families and children under the age of four get in free.

Cabacera Park itself is a great place for walks and there are some super photo opportunities from the special viewpoint. There is a lake where gentle trips on the water can be taken in boats shaped like giant swans which is great for families with children. As well as a bar and children's play area there is an open air auditorium where live performances are held.

Cathedral

Plaza Almoina, s/n
46003
Valencia
Tel: +34 963 918 127
www.catedraldevalencia.es

Construction on the cathedral in Valencia started at the end of the 13th century and the building is predominantly Gothic although other architectural styles have been added. The cathedral has undergone several periods of renovation over its lifetime and currently is in remarkably good condition. The highlights inside the cathedral are the Chapel of the Holy Grail and the star motifs of the vault. Amongst numerous objects on display inside is a goblet from the first century AD, which is a relic from the Holy Grail.

Walking down the wide and airy nave leads you to the rather ornate but beautiful altarpiece with its Renaissance frescoes. On the outside the cathedral features two incredibly old doors, the Puerta del Palau is the oldest with Mudéjar elements in the Romanesque style and the Door of the Apostles is from the 15th century. The bell tower has eleven bells; some use an automated process to mark the hour and some can be rung manually. The bells in Valencia Cathedral are the largest group of Gothic bells in Spain.

In the Middle Ages King James I of Spain set up a council to administer the distribution of the water from the Turia river to local farmers. The council, Tribunal de las Aguas, survives to this day and the eight selected local farmers still meet every Thursday at midday at Valencia Cathedral. The meetings are in Valencian, the local language, and their word is law as far as irrigation and anything to do with the distribution of water goes. The Tribunal de las Aguas has been awarded the Intangible Cultural Heritage of Humanity by UNESCO.

The cathedral is open from 20th March until 31st October, Monday to Saturday from 10am to 6.30pm, Sundays and public holidays from 2pm to 6.30pm. From 1st November to 19th March, the hours are Monday to Saturday 10am to 5.30pm. The general admission price is €3 for adults and €2.10 for concessions. A guided tour is also available with audio guides available in many different languages.

Silk Market (La Lonja de Seda)

Plaza del Mercado
46001
Valencia
Tel: +34 963 153 931

The building that houses the Silk Market in Valencia is considered to be the most beautiful Gothic building in the country and has been declared by UNESCO as a world heritage site.

This masterpiece of Gothic architecture doesn't give any clue from the outside as to the true nature of the business that was carried on inside. Many people think the building might be a castle as there is a huge tower; others think it maybe a church because of the ornately decorated door. Not many people would guess that that the origins of the building were as the local silk exchange.

During the 15th century the economy of Valencia was growing rapidly as the port meant that connections to other places in the world were relatively easy. The businessmen in the city needed somewhere to meet and make their deals according to their social status and so the Silk Market was built.

The vaulted ceiling in the main hall is supported by twisted columns which seem to stretch upwards forever from the marbled floor. The decoration is lavish and this style continues out into the garden with its orange trees and grotesque gargoyles. There are two other rooms in the compound and over the years these have served as courts as well as a prison and also as residences for city officials. In one of these rooms the tiling on the floor is intriguing and has an almost 3D effect.

Opening hours are Tuesday to Saturday 10am to 2pm and 4:30pm to 8:30pm, Sundays and public holidays 10am to 3pm and closed Mondays. Admission prices are €2 for adults and €1 for children and senior citizens.

Central Market

Plaza del Mercado
46001
Valencia
Tel: +34 963 829 100
www.mercadocentralvalencia.es/

The Central Market will take your breath away as there are 400 hundred stalls spread out over two floors in this modern steel, glass and stone structure. Despite the modern materials the Central Market building is attractive with arched windows and doors and the roof is topped off with a central dome. The interior is big, bright and airy and well organised so everything is easy to find.

The stalls are laden with freshly picked and brightly coloured produce and it is easy to see why the Spanish shop daily with such bounty on their doorstep. The mingling smells of spices, exotic fruits and vegetables, fish, meats and flowers can be a heady perfume as you join in the hustle and bustle of the Valencianos doing their daily shopping. There are numerous tapas bars and cafeterias inside and outside the market building where after a busy morning of haggling it is great to have a coffee and watch the world go by.The market is open Monday to Saturday from 7am to 2pm.

Serranos Towers

Plaza de los Fueros 46003 Valencia
Tel: +34 963 919 070

The Serranos Towers date from the Middle Ages and are one of twelve gates built as access points in the city wall. Designed by Pere Balaguer, a master stonemason, the actual gateway is a semi-circular arch with a pentagonal shaped structure either side. Only two of the twelve gates remain now and the Serranos Towers only survived the removal of the city wall in 1865 as they were in use as a prison for knights and noblemen. The towers are considered to be one of the landmarks of Valencia and are well worth a visit for their elegant Gothic style and sheer size. There are different levels which can be walked through all the way to the top from which there are stunning views across the city. The Serranos Towers are open Tuesday to Saturday from 10am to 6pm, with slightly longer hours in the summer. On Sunday and public holidays the gates open from 10am to 3pm but the admission is free. General admission is €2 and concessions pay just €1.

City of Arts & Sciences

Avda. del Professor López Piñero & C/ Eduardo Primo Yúfera 46013 Valencia
Tel: +34 902 100 031
www.cac.es/

The City of Arts and Sciences in Valencia is an amazing sight and to see all this complex has to offer can take more than one day.

The different areas of Hemisfèric, the Principe Felipe Science Museum, Oceangràfic, Palau de les Arts, Umbracle and Ágora offer opportunities to get to know the varying aspects of art, science, nature and technology.

In general the different areas open at 10am each day and close at 6pm, at weekends and in high season the closing times are slightly later. Each area has its own website link with admission prices and timetables of any special shows or performances. There is on-site car parking underneath the Umbracle but the public transport system is excellent with bus and train stops nearby.

There are plenty of places to eat and drink within the complex; pizzerias, burger bars, ice cream parlour's, a 750 seater self-service restaurant and the beautiful Submarino Restaurant where you can dine surrounded by 10,000 fish.

Hemisfèric Cinema

www.cac.es/hemisferic/

For cinema lovers this is definitely the place to go. The concave screen is the largest in Spain and measures 900 square metres or nearly 3000 square feet. There is a varied timetable with films for children and adults, local information documentaries and nature programmes.

Science Museum Príncipe Felipe

www.cac.es/museo/

This is a true 21st century science museum and uses didactic and interactive means to encourage visitors to understand our wonderful world of technology, science and the environment. Since its inauguration in 2000 over 27 million visitors have passed through its doors and been amused and surprised by this forward thinking museum.

The museum is on three floors, with the shops, restaurants and ticket offices on the ground floor. This level is free to the public and there are many exhibitions held in here each year.

On the first floor there are science exhibitions, many of which are interactive, and workshops where visitors can experiment with modules like "Exploratorium" and "Furnishing the World". A giant representation of a DNA helix can be seen as well as a Foucault Pendulum, one of the longest in the world at 110 feet. The pendulum is a simple device and demonstrates the rotation of the Earth.

From the top level of the museum there are spectacular views out over the Turia river park and children can have fun trying to count the 4,000 panes of glass that make up the museum building.

Oceanogràfic Aquarium

www.cac.es/oceanografic/

Oceanogràfic in Valencia represents individuals from all of the world's main ecosystems and is the largest aquarium in Europe. In the Dolphinarium alone there are over there are 24 million litres of water. Across the whole site there are 500 different species: penguins, sharks, sea lions, turtles, manta rays, belugas, star fish, jelly fish and many others, as well as crustaceans of all types. Around 45,000 individuals swim, float and play in this aquatic environment.

The journey around the various buildings takes visitors past sheer glass walls where you can get up close and personal with the penguins and a walk through the glass tunnel where sharks swim overhead is almost as good as being in the water with them. There are examples of tropical mangrove swamps, and a bit closer to home, the Albufera de Valencia and its wetland bird species.

For those all-important souvenirs there are several gift shops in Oceanogràfic selling a variety of marine related items as well as sweets and snacks. In the Dolphin shop there are 500 products all with a dolphin theme and in the Arctic Bazaar the theme is penguins and Beluga whales as well as many other animals that call the Arctic and Antarctic home.

Palau de les Arts

www.cac.es/palau/

The Valencia region has a privileged position in the world of culture and musical traditions and the Palau de les Arts has been constructed with this in mind. This modern space has the latest state of the art technology so whether you prefer to listen to opera singers or watch a ballet or enjoy a classical music performance, perfect sound is guaranteed.

Many major artists have performed here and a lot of these have been attracted by the leadership of Helga Schmidt who from 1973 to 1981 held a similar position at London's Royal Opera House. The Valencian Community Orchestra is the resident orchestra at the Queen Sofia Palace of the Arts and their first season was 2006-2007. Most seasons they perform seven or eight operas and a zarzuela. There are occasionally operettas and vocal recitals as well.

In 2007 Plácido Domingo bought his Operalia competition to Valencia and even now puts on regular performances. Opera galas, vocal recitals and symphonic performances are promoted by the Queen Sofia company and there is an advanced training programme for young artists. The Centre de Perfeccionament for these young people is named in honor of Plácido Domingo.

Umbracle (City of Arts & Sciences)

www.cac.es/umbracle/

The Umbracle brings together all the areas of the City of Arts and Sciences and there are exhibition zones as well as walkways and lakes plus plenty of landscaped areas to sit and relax in. The Umbracle does a brilliant job in disguising the car park underneath and it is a pleasure to take a leisurely stroll and admire the fantastic vegetation representing the best that Mediterranean gardening has to offer.

Within the four or so acres of lush foliage and shady corners there is an Art Promenade with some very interesting sculptures by international artists. There is also a Garden Of Astronomy which complements the activities held in the Science Museum and this is an open access area for everyone to enjoy.

Ágora Events Arena

www.cac.es/agora/

This multi-functional space is used for exhibitions, conferences, sports events, concerts and performances. Since its inauguration, various major events have been held at the Àgora including the Valencia Open 500 Tennis Tournament, Fashion Week and the Freestyle Burn Spanish Cup with both national and international riders taking part.

In the weeks leading up to Christmas there is plenty going on with a full programme of parties and shows for children plus an ice skating rink.

Museum of Enlightenment & Modernity

Calle de Quevedo, 10, 46001 Valencia
Tel: +34 963 883 730
www.muvim.es

The Valencia Museum of Enlightenment and Modernity or MuVIM focuses on the history of media from the 17th century to the present day. There are permanent exhibitions as well as many temporary ones and workshops, courses, lectures and seminars are offered to complement these. There is a cafeteria, bookshop and shop and the opening times are Tuesday to Saturday 10am to 2pm and 4pm to 8pm, Sunday 10am to 2pm.

Monastery San Miguel de los Reyes

Avinguda de la Constitució, 284
46019 Valencia
Tel: + 34 963 874 000
www.bv.gva.es/

A short distance from the city centre is this former monastery. It is built in the Renaissance style and the inner yard with its arches is a wonderfully tranquil place to rest awhile.

This beautiful building was built in the 16th century on the site of an old abbey and was looked after and loved until 1859. It was then used as a prison right up until the 1950's. A period of neglect followed until the monastery was restored and brought back into use.

The monastery sits in front of a marbled square, quite alone apart from a few gently waving palm trees. A visit here is an incredible experience which will leave a lasting impression, especially if the sun is setting during your visit casting a red glow across the beautiful stonework.

The building is now the headquarters of Valencia Library and home to the Valencian Language Academy, the Valencia Property Registry and the Directorate General of Books, Archives and Libraries.

A guided tour is available and this gives access to the church, crypt and the North wing. The guided tours are by prior appointment and are on Tuesday, Saturday, Sunday and public holidays. If you choose to wander alone access is restricted to the outside of this magnificent building and the South wing. The hours for this are Tuesday to Friday 10am to 2pm and 5pm to 8pm, Saturday, Sunday and public holidays 11am to 1.30pm. Admission is free as are the guided tours.

Palacio del Marques de Dos Aguas & Museo Nacional de Cerámica González Martí

Calle del Poeta Querol, 2, 46002 Valencia
Tel: +34 963 516 392
www.mnceramica.mcu.es/

The Dos Aguas (Two Waters) in the name refers to Valencia's two main rivers and these are represented by two voluptuous male figures outside the door to this flamboyant Rococo palace. Along with these two oversized figures the main door is surrounded by the intricate alabaster carvings of fruit and vegetables.

Since 1954 the palace has housed the Ceramics Museum and this is an impressive collection where much can be learnt about the history of Valencia and its inhabitants. There is a Valencian kitchen where everything has been created out of ceramics and some fine examples of carriages that are so ornate it is hard to imagine them ever been used.

The admission fee for the palace and Ceramics Museum together is €3 for general entry and €1.50 for concessions. Entry is free on Saturday from 4pm to 8pm and on a Sunday. The opening times are Tuesday to Saturday 10am to 2pm and 4pm to 8pm. On Sunday and public holidays the hours are 10am to 2pm, closed all day Monday.

Church of Saint John Hospital

Calle del Trinquete de Caballeros
46003 Valencia
Tel: +34 963 922 965
www.sanjuandelhospital.es

This historic church was constructed in the 13th century and was the first church to be built in the city after Valencia Cathedral. The land the church stands on was donated by James I and the Gothic and Baroque style church is dedicated to Saint John the Baptist. The site of the church used to be a hospital which is where the name comes from; the Jerusalem Order of the Hospital of Rhodes and of Malta.

The church has a single nave with chapels on either side and there are many 13th century frescoes and an interesting 16th century altarpiece. The church has suffered periods of neglect and has been lucky to survive demolition; it was only by the intervention of the Second Vatican Council that recovery work began. The work is still not completed and many thousands of Valencianos are supporting the restoration work with the aim of bringing the church back to its original splendour, some 700 years after it was first constructed.

The Prelature of Opus Dei are in charge of the church now and a full programme of worship is available as the church in general sees increasing activity in both interest and attendance levels. Services can be arranged in German, English and Dutch as well as Spanish.

The general opening hours are Monday to Friday 7am to 8am, 9.30am to 1.30pm, and 5pm to 9pm. Saturday 9.30 to 1.30pm and 5pm to 9pm and Sunday 11pm to 2pm and 5pm to 9pm.

Almoina Archaelogical Museum

Plaza Decimus Junius Brutus (CONSOL Rome), s/n 46001 Valencia
Tel: +34 962 084 173

The Almoina Museum is fascinating as it has been built on the site where the ruins were discovered. Cleverly designed glass walkways protect the historical treasures that lie beneath but still allow visitors to see the wonders of this great find. The foundations that were uncovered have been left exactly as they were and a vast glass floor has laid over them so it is easy to get an understanding of the layout of the building exactly as it was two thousand years ago.

Many items of great historical significance have been found here and a tour of the museum gives an excellent insight into Valencia's history. Visitors can see the ruins of several ceremonial buildings, two Roman streets and a patio from an ancient Muslin city. There is an excellent example of a Roman spa from the 2nd century B.C. including a nearly complete Roman bath.

The entry fee of €2 is well worth it and if you choose to visit on a Sunday or public holiday between 10am and 3pm entry is free. The rest of the week the museum is open Tuesday to Saturday 10am to 6pm, with slightly longer hours in the summer months.

Recommendations for the Budget Traveller

Places to Stay

There is no shortage of cozy and budget-friendly places to stay in Valencia, no matter the season you decide to visit. Some will want to stay in the part of the city closest to the Cathedral, where the most shops, bars, and restaurants are concentrated, but you'll find Valencia extremely accessible even if you stay outside the Old City boundary. In any case, you'd be surprised how many places are affordable and can be found in close proximity to all the activities and main attractions.

Purple Nest Hostel

The Purple Nest Hostel is one of the best budget-friendly hostels in the city, and boasts the largest communal kitchen in any of the hostels in Valencia. It is part of a chain, which helps in guaranteeing a certain level of service and also fairness in pricing. The beds and furniture are all relatively new, having been renovated in the last few years. As an added bonus, it is located right in the center of town, close to the Turia Gardens and main shopping and restaurant streets. Price for a night will vary according to season, but will not be more than 60 Euros.

Address: Plaza Tetuán, 5, 46003, Valencia
Telephone: +34 963 532 561
www.nesthostelsvalencia.com/purple

Hotel Petit Germanias

Hotel Petit Germanias Valencia is a very affordable three-star boutique hotel which is located in the heart of Old Town. This hotel offers incredible value for your money, has free internet, and also has a bed-and-breakfast option that is very affordable. Prices, according to season, can range from 50-70 Euros per night, breakfast included.

Address: C/ Sueca, 14 46006 Valencia
Telephone: +34 963 513 638
http://www.hthoteles.com/es/hotel-petit-palace-germanias-valencia/

Petit Palace Bristol Hotel

Petit Palace Bristol Hotel is located right next to the Cathedral, right in the center of Old Town. You would be hard-pressed to find a hotel with such high quality at such an affordable price. This hotel has free internet, some rooms with terraces, and a beautiful lounge where you can catch a drink before your big night out. You should expect to pay from 50-70 Euros per night here, depending on the season.

Address: Calle de la Abadía de San Martín, 3, Valencia
Telephone: + 34 963 94 51 00
www.petitpalacebristolhotel.com/

Medium Hotels

Medium Hotels is a chain of moderately priced hotels in Spain. The Medium Hotel in Valencia has more than 150 rooms, a pool, free wifi, and several lounges and breakfast rooms. There's also a Mediterranean restaurant right on the premises, in case you're too tired to hop outside and traipse around town. This hotel is also special because it has several promotions that you can opt for on its website, including all-inclusive packages with breakfast or tours. You may even want to choose the "Bicycle" package to tour around Old Town on a bicycle for three hours one morning. Expect to spend around 50-70 Euros per night, depending on the season.

Address: General Urrutia, 48, 46013
Telephone: +34 963 34 78 00
https://www.mediumhoteles.com/

Eating & Drinking

Come to Valencia, and you will not go hungry. From fresh fish plucked from the Sea to huge portions of Paella prepared slowly over a low heat, you will not be disappointed at the culinary variety you will find here. Here are some places not to miss.

Restaurante La Santa Compana

Restaurante La Santa Compana is a great choice for a wide variety of food, not just your local fare. Expect to come here and enjoy a juicy steak, or other specials the chef may decide to whip up. This restaurant also boasts an *enoteca*, a section of the restaurant you can order a more casual meal with some delicious local wine. Price: 20 Euros per person.

Address: Calle Roteros 21, El Carmen, Valencia
Telephone: +34 963922259

Restaurante L'Estimat

Restaurante L'Estimat is the place to get your Paella.

To get the best "local" experience, go at lunchtime where you'll share a table and maybe even a dish or two with the residents. There are other fresh dishes to choose from, and you won't be disappointed with the seafood, or the view. This treasure is located right on the sea. Price: 20-30 Euros per person.

Address: Avda. Neptuno 16, Playa de las Arenas, Valencia
Telephone: +34 96 371 10 18
http://www.restaurantelestimat.com/eng/index.htm

Lambrusqueria

Lambrusqueria is the place to go for Mediterranean food of the Italian variety. It's tucked away in the center of town, and has both indoor and outdoor seating. Even though their specialties include pasta and salad, you'll also want to try some Tapas for some local flair.

Address: Calle Conde Altea 31, Valencia
Telephone: +34 963340753
http://lambrusqueria.wordpress.com/

La Bodeguilla del Gato

La Bodeguilla del Gato serves perhaps the best Tapas in town. Walk into this small bodega and you are bathed in the brightest orange walls you've ever seen – smothered with everything from Renaissance paintings, wooden spoons, and a bicycle. Go and expect to order a lot more than you originally planned, as the menu is just that good. Open until 2 am, you may end up staying for more than the food, as the atmosphere gets more relaxed and vibrant as the night goes on. At the weekend, plan on calling ahead to make a reservation.

Address: Calle de Catalans, 10
46001, Valencia
Telephone: +34 963 918 235

L'Umbracle Terraza

Spend all day in the City of Arts and Sciences? Don't think you need to get back to city center or the beach to have a good time. One of Valencia's best new bars is here, and has a great variety of tapas, cocktails, and a gorgeous terrace where you can dance the night away.

Address: Avda. del Saler 5,
City of Arts and Sciences, Valencia
Telephone: + 34 607 659 705
http://www.umbracleterraza.com

Casa Montana

After dinner, head down to this small, cozy wine and cocktail bar for some drinks before hitting the town. It is known for its excellent Spanish wine collection, and the bartenders are the perfect balance of knowledgeable and modest. Seats fill up quickly, but it's equally fun to be up at the beautiful wooden bar, watching the bartenders work their magic.

Address: Calle de José Benlliure, 69, Valencia
Telephone: + 34 963 67 23 14
www.emilianobodega.com

Carmen Neighborhood

If you're looking for a night out you certainly will never forget, look no further than within the confines of the old city, in the old, winding streets behind the Cathedral. This is where you can best experience the melting pot of Valencia for yourself, as everyone, no matter your race, age, class, or creed, finds a bar or club to hang out here. It is definitely the "alternative neighborhood" of Valencia, but the variety of locals it offers has something for everyone.

For the most bars and clubs, head to the area between the Torres de Serranos and the Plaza de la Virgen; this is where the nightlife is most concentrated. While many bars and clubs will be absolutely worth your while, you may want to try out **Radio City, Pinball, Mitjanit, and Bigornia** as some of the local favorites. Most of these clubs close at around 4 am, so be prepared to close up and head to the beach, or into Carmen for some late-night action.

For a complete listing of clubs and bars, go here: http://www.valenciavalencia.com/nightlife-guide/carmen/carmen-nightlife.htm

Shopping

Whether you're in Valencia for the beautiful beaches, for the tapas, for the Flamenco, or for the dusk-till-dawn nightlife, you'll absolutely need a break to shop. Or at least you should take a break to shop, whether for a ripe orange or for a new pair of Manolos, as this town has more shops you can visit in a lifetime.

While you're here, though, best to follow the local daily schedule, and expect shops to be closed during most of the afternoon hours, particularly from 1pm to around 4 or 5pm. This is when the town takes a *siesta*, or afternoon nap, and you should too, if you plan on having the night you should here.

Valencia is like many Spanish towns, where many stores are clustered along several streets or in a certain neighborhood. The following is a list of some great places to start. Of course, the best way to find your favorite shop is to get lost: wander in the alleyways behind the cathedral, along the old riverbed and the ancient walls of the city. You'll be surprised what treasures you may find.

El Corte Ingles

This Spanish institution is a one-stop-shop for just about anything you want to find from a department store. Need an extra bathing costume for the beach? Need to pick up a new pair of shoes, or sunglasses? Head to one of this store's many locations to pick up whatever you might need for a great price. Check the website for the most convenient store to your location:
http://www.elcorteingles.es/

Calle La Pau & Calle Marques de Dos Aigue

These two streets in the center of town are the places to go if you fancy shopping local names like Carolina Herrera, and also the international design super-stars like Prada or Versace. These streets can be a bit more expensive but if you search you will find a bargain hidden in the designer aisles. These streets are also ideal if your idea of a perfect afternoon is window-shopping and people-watching: the designs you'll see even just walking down these streets will make your eyes pop.

Valencia F.C. Shop at the Train Station

Your eyebrows may be raised, but this is the place to go to buy your Valencia F.C. Merchandise. Inside the train station is city's official store to find anything in support of the local football club.

Calle Don Juan de Austria & Calle Colon

These are the best streets to wander down if you're not too into the designer scene but you're more into the mid-range stores like H&M, Desigual, and Mango. These two streets run into each other, so if you hit one, you're not far from the other.

Teashop

If you want to get your friends and family a unique gift, stop by this boutique store to buy any assortment of tea, or create your own special blend. The shopkeepers are nice and welcoming, and are in no way snobbish about their teas, so ask away, and come away with a souvenir that will last you months to come.

Address: Calle de Jorge Juan, 1, Valencia
Telephone: 963 517 722
http://www.teashop.es/

Benidorm, Alicante & Costa Blanca

The Costa Blanca is a holiday paradise on the Mediterranean coast of Spain. One of the most popular vacation destinations in Europe, the Costa Blanca appeals with its long coastline, sunny beaches and Iberian culture.

From the northern city of Dénia to the southern town of Guardarmar, Costa Blanca presents its guests with an array of superlative entertainments, and invites its guests to stay a while, explore the sights, and drink wine in the fading glow of a Mediterranean sunset.

Costa Blanca is a part of the extravagant Valencian province of Alicante; and the two cities in this region of note are Benidorm and the city of Alicante. The latter is the capital city of the province of Alicante, and an epicenter for delightful entertainment, stunning views of the Mediterranean, and a rich Spanish culture. Alicante, an old Mediterranean fort and fishing village, is the second largest Valencian city in the region and one of the most rapidly growing cities in all of Spain. The historic city boasts a decadent castle, an assortment of artistically designed parks, and a unique architecture.

Benidorm is a picturesque city in the Alicante Mountains, offering spectacular views of the sea from various points both high and low throughout the region. Yet, in spite of its old world charm, Benidorm is a rising modern city and one of the most popular destination spots in all of Spain. Whether you like to boat, hike, immerse yourself in history, or relax in full view of the magnificent Sea, Costa Blanca is a coastal paradise that can provide all the entertainment beauty you desire while vacation.

Culture

Costa Blanca contains both the historic allure of centuries pasts and the exciting development of modern style and entertainment. In the towns of Alicante and Benidorm you can find ancient castles and monuments alongside disco pubs and cabaret bars. It has one of the most exuberant nightlife scenes in all of Spain, and its location near the sprawling beach makes it a sought after destination for people all over the world looking to have some fun in the sand. Although evidences of its unique religious history are everywhere, it has its origins in Catholicism, the evolution of the city has turned it into a coastal metropolis where freedom and expression are the only required fundamentals. There is an accessibility to Alicante and Benidorm that is usually tucked away in most places, people who come here know that they will be able to let loose, and to not worry about the busy lives they left at home.

The region has developed extensively over the last few decades, and is now home to a diversity of unique architecture, an array of brilliantly organized museums, and a thrilling music scene. A trip to Costa Blanca does not automatically imply a week on the beach, or afternoons spent looking at ruins, with nothing else to do. There are theme parks, traditional and modern musical entertainment, comedy shows, and water sports. And more, the people of Costa Blanca are part of a culture of freedom. They know how to have fun, and make it possible so you can too.

Location & Orientation

Extending for 200 miles along the majestic Mediterranean coast, Costa Blanca is an extensive paradise on the west coast of Spain. The territory spans from Dénia in the north to Guardarmar in the South, and contains the popular destinations of Benidorm and Alicante within its vast region. It is a relatively mountainous area speckled with picturesque villages in full view of the Sea.

The cities of Benidorm and Alicante are situated in the province of Alicante within the region of Costa Blanca. Benidorm is more mountainous than its neighbor Alicante, but both have stunning coastlines in their possession. The most prominent mountain in the region is Mount Benacantil, but it is small by many standards, rising to an elevation of just 169 meters. It is easy to access Costa Blanca by plane, train, or boat, but book early, as this is a very popular place to visit, especially in the rich summer months.

Climate & When to Visit

The region of Costa Blanca possesses a subtropical climate that remains moderate, inviting visitors to come and bask in the nearby salubrious seas of the Mediterranean, and to enjoy the radiant light of the Spanish sun. The summers in Costa Blanca are enduring, sturdy, and the temperatures remain warm for several months out of the year.

Temperatures can be as high as 40 degrees Celsius in summer, but average at about 30 degrees Celsius from May through mid-October. Costa Blanca is also an extremely long extension, so various parts of the territory have differing temperatures throughout the year. But generally, the best time to visit Costa Blanca is in May or June, before the weather becomes too warm and the tourists have yet to arrive. Although in September and October the air is considerably cooler than its preceding summer months, it is the predominant wet season in Costa Blanca as a result of the "cold drop" that has a tendency to cause severe flooding. Yet, in spite of this unusual typicality, Costa Blanca only sees 35-40 rainy days per year on average.

In the province of Alicante, in the cities of Benidorm and Alicante, the story is similar. Because of its providential location to the lush Mediterranean Sea, the region benefits from a cooling trend in summer and a warming one in winter. In Benidorm, because of its situation within the Alicante Mountains, temperatures remain cooler throughout the year, and the area tends to have a distinct climate from the rest of the region. In the town of Alicante the temperature is milder, with temperatures ranging from 6-18 degrees Celsius in winter, and 17-30 degrees Celsius in summer. The province of Alicante is truly in its height of glory at the end of spring, when the summer sun has yet to blare down, and the new year's freshness of the Mediterranean still lingers along the Costa Blanca.

Sightseeing Highlights

Visit the Old City of Valencia

Along the radiant Mediterranean Sea three hours west of Madrid, Spain lies the magnificent old city of Valencia. It is the third largest metropolis in the Spanish mainland, and by all accounts, a true international city. Valencia was founded by the Romans during the second century and has contained the largest seaport in all of Spain.

Valencia is a town steeped in history, with a rich culture of art, music, and architecture to accompany it. The city possesses spectacular views, ancient monuments, and contemporary art showcases within its territories. The most significant monuments include the <u>Cathedral of Valencia, City of Arts and Sciences</u>, and UNESCO world heritage site <u>Llotja de la Seda </u>(Silk Exchange). The reason why the latter building contains such a wealth of world significance is because it is a prime example of a non-religious building in late Gothic style, thus making the structure a standing tribute to the power of the former Mediterranean mercantile city of Valencia.

Valencia is located in a region of Spain called the Costa del Azahar, the Orange Blossom Coast, which has been an area dedicated to industry for the past hundred years. But Valencia stands alone in the territory as a breathtaking living memory of the Spain of centuries ago. Valencia had been part of this push towards industrial development until the mid-1990s when the beauty and world importance of this grand city was recognized. Now, a visit to Valencia is a step into the old world, into a bustling epicenter of art, culture, and energy,

Casco Antiguo, Benidorm

Benidorm, Costa Blanca, Spain

Although the city of Benidorm has seen an influx of tourism that, in most cases, tends to destroy the luxurious simplicity of picturesque towns, Benidorm has managed to retain the integrity and the charm of its Spanish heritage. Authentic Spanish culture in Benidorm is cradled in the old town, the Casco Antiguo, of the region - the official epicenter of ancient art, culture, and genuine Spanish influence in the city. Along the beaches you may find the sprawling evidence of modern society, but Casco Antiguo offers a glimpse into the Costa Blanca of long ago.

There are four main attractions at Casco Antiguo that you can't miss during your stay in Benidorm: the Castillo y Mirador, the Church of San Jaime, the Maritime Cultural Center, and Plaza Mayor. Guests are encouraged to wander through the quaint cobblestone streets, delight in the views of the surrounding coast, and enjoy the history that is evident in the area of Casco Antiguo.

The Castillo y Mirador is called the Balcony of the Mediterranean, and extends from an old fortress that no longer stands, allowing guests a closer look at the beautiful sea. The Church of San Jaime is an 18th century jewel of Costa Blanca with minimalist decor, but the most transcendent of atmospheres. The Maritime Cultural Center is housed in a small villa with various exhibitions of the unique fishing and boating history of Benidorm's past. Entrance to the center is free. Plaza Mayor is a labyrinthine center of activity offering a variety of entertainment, shopping, and food.

Island of Tabarca, Alicante

The largest inhabited island in the region of Costa Blanca, the Island of Tabarca in Alicante, is a stunning representation of the beauty of the region, and an exciting excursion to take on your stay in Costa Blanca. Tabarca, or "the flat island," has a strong Genoese history. The Island was invaded by a Tunisian king in the 18th century and captured the Genoan citizenry of the island. They weren't released until 20 years later, it was then that they fortified the island from threats from the sea.

Now, the island is not only a protected marine reserve, but a destination offering some of the most eye catching architecture in Costa Blanca and the best seafood available. On the island lies the Church of Saint Peter and Paul, a baroque style cathedral that can be seen from the opposite Spanish coast. Other important sites on the island are the Church of Saint Joseph and the Governor's House, now a hotel. These are housed in the center of the island, and the area has been declared a Protected Historic Artistic monument.

The Isle of Tabarca possesses an ecologically significant posidonia (flowering underwater plants) prairie, a fact which led to the preservation of the water around the island. This particular prairie is the largest in the Spanish Mediterranean. Visitors are encouraged to snorkel and scuba dive along the colorful reef, or to relax in the abundant sunshine of the coast.

The Ferry to the island departs from Alicante Marina and takes approximately one hour. Round trip price is €14 - €20. Phone number for the operator is +34 965 216 396.

Catch the Sun at Playa de Poniente, Benidorm

One of the most popular, and arguably the most beautiful, beaches on Spain's White Coast is the exquisite Playa de Poniente in Benidorm. The beach at Playa de Poniente extends for 2 miles and contains exquisite views of the sparkling Mediterranean and the stunning distant Alicante Mountains. Its length begins in the Old Town of Benidorm at Casco Antiguo and ends at the Cala de Finestrat.

The beaches in Costa Blanca have a reputation for being busy but clean. There are people charged with maintaining this level of quality who work at night, so that in the morning the beach is fresh and new. Also, they possess some of the most spectacular views in the region. Poniente Beach (Playa de Ponienta) especially is known for its exquisite sand and depth of beach area. The vast beach meets luxurious ocean in a breathtaking display of natural wonder at Poniente Beach.

Also, if you're looking to avoid the bustling crowds in Costa Blanca near the water, Poniente Beach is the best place to be. For various reasons, Poniente Beach tends to be less busy than a majority of the other beaches in the area. Also, this beach offers an assortment of sun beds for guests so you can enjoy some sun in comfort while working on your tan.

The beach operates like a public park and is open in summer from 9:00 am to 8:00 pm, and in winter from 10:00 am to 5:00 pm in association with local daylight hours.

The Castle of Santa Bárbara, Alicante

03002 Alicante, Spain
+965 263 131

Standing atop the impressive Mount Benacantil in the Alicante Mountains, the Castle of Santa Bárbara is an ancient fortress that showcases the incredible history of Costa Blanca. Situated on a cliff overlooking the historic city, the Castle of Santa Bárbara is one of the largest medieval castles on the European continent, and it can be seen from miles away.

The structure was built in the 10th century by the Moors, but was overtaken by King Alfonse of the Castilian people in the 13th on December 4th, Saint Bárbara's Day. And because it was on this Saint's day that the King earned his victory, he named the castle after her. It was later captured by James of Aragon. It was involved in a series of wars over the next few hundred years, until it fell into disuse at the latter part of the 19th century.

For almost a hundred years, it sat unheeded atop the mountain in Costa Blanca; but in 1963 it was recognized as an important historical structure, renovated, and opened to the public. There have even been elevators built into the rock. The fortress sports cannons, palace quarters, dungeons, and spectacular views of Alicante around the grounds.

The castle is completely free to the public and has two entrances. Much of the area is steep, so make sure you wear appropriate footwear. But, for your convenience, the fortress is equipped with two cafés, so if you become hungry or thirsty on your excursion you don't have to go without.

Aqualandia Water Park, Benidorm

Sierra Helada s/n, Rincón de Loix 03503
Benidorm, Alicante, Spain
+965 86 01 00
http://www.aqualandia.net/

You've brought your family along with you to the wonderland that is Costa Blanca, you've seen the ruins and the sights, eaten in the best of restaurants, what's left for you to do? Go to a theme park of course! A water theme park exists in the city of Benidorm that is fun for the entire family. It is a place to cool down, to enjoy the sun in luxury along the waterside. Whether you want to lounge in the shade or take part in the various activities throughout the park, a day at Aqualandia is one of the best ways to beat the heat on vacation in Costa Blanca.

Aqualandia offers a different way to spend an afternoon or two while visiting Costa Blanca. Don't settle for an evening by the boring hotel pool when you can have an adventure at Aqualandia. And if you have children they will absolutely love you for taking them to this incredible water park.

The theme park also contains various amenities such as sun beds and lockers. In addition to providing for your basic needs, they also have a large food court that is relatively inexpensive for being attached to a theme park. The rides vary in intensity, offering fun options for kids of all ages.

Admission to the park is €25, but discount tickets are available at various places. Also, if you plan on visiting multiple parks during your stay in Costa Blanca, there are great deals on multi park tickets available as well.

Mundomar, Benidorm

Sierra Helada - Rincón de Loix
Benidorm, Spain
+965 860 100
http://www.mundomar.es/

Mundomar is a remarkable theme park that centers around animal life, but offers so much more to visitors than the typical zoo experience. There are dozens of exhibits and sprawling gardens containing a myriad of species from all over the world.

Guest are encouraged to stroll in the green spaces, attend live animal shows, and even swim with dolphins. The areas of the park include exotic and rare birds, mammals, unusual and adorable aquatic life, and much more.

One of the best reviewed shows that takes place within the park is the live show with sea lions. It is comedic entertainment coupled centered around the magnificent animals. In addition to the shows, guests are able to swim with sea lions as well. No matter what your age, you're sure to have a blast at Mundomar. The gardens are spectacular, the animals are exciting, and there's fun to be had around every corner. It's a great way to spend a day while on vacation in Costa Blanca.

Entrance to the park is €18.5 for adults and €16.5 for children. If you wish to swim with dolphins, prices are set at €90 for adults and €65 for children. For sea lions it is €30. Advance tickets can be bought for discount prices as well.

Terra Mitica, Benidorm

03502 Benidorm, Spain
+ 965 004 300
http://www.terramiticapark.com/

One of the most exciting themes parks in Costa Blanca, Terra Mitica offers a unique experience that's an interesting addition to any visit here. There are five main zones within the park: Egypt, Greece, Rome, Iberia, and the Islands, each with their own particular fascinations and entertainment.

A visit to Terra Mitica is like a concentrated tour of the best parts of the Mediterranean, like you're taking micro trip into each of the various regions.

The 25 rides available at the park offer the best of entertainment to contemporary thrill seekers. The park is home to the largest wooden roller coaster in Europe, the Magnus Colossus, at 36 meters high. Also featured at Terra Mitica is La Furia de Tritón, a themed boat drop thrill ride that's as exhilarating as it is alluring. Each zone has its own main attraction, all of them based off of real landmarks found in the ancient world territories.

The park also hosts a wide array of entertaining shows which are both educational and comedic. Traditional Mediterranean song and dance performances combine with legends from the past, showcasing the unique histories of the regions. You can travel through Egypt with archeologists, meet ancient gods, or even take part in a disco.

Admission to the park is €34 for adults, and children under 5 can enter the park for free.

Hiking in the Alicante Mountains

The impressive Alicante Mountains are some of the most beautiful formations in Costa Blanca, lining the coasts and adding to the splendor of the region. The summits of this range are not as high as many in Europe, offering a chance to the average hiker to reach the mountaintops without much difficulty.

A hike in the Alicante Mountains are more akin to a stroll through nature, but in Costa Blanca visitors are offered spectacular views of the cities below and the surrounding sea. From the tops of the Alicante Mountains, you can see for miles - the breathtaking valley below becomes complete within your sights.

The most prominent mountain in Costa Blanca is Mount Benacantil, home to the famous Castle of Saint Bárbara. But this is just one of many destinations. The trails in the Alicante mountains are safe, and visitors are encouraged to wander at their leisure. The panorama of Costa Blanca spreads out beneath you, creating easily accessible picture perfect opportunities.

There are treks for more advanced hikers in the Alicante mountains as well, depending on which trail you follow you can be able to climb rock faces, and discover hidden caves and water falls. The beauty of Costa Blanca is at your fingertips in these mountains. It is up to you to choose how far you wish to explore. Whether you wish to take an easy afternoon hike, or a more serious trek, the Alicante Mountains are a perfect place to be one with great outdoors in Costa Blanca.

Terra Natura, Benidorm

Partida Foia del Verdader 1, 03502
Benidorm, Alicante, Spain
+966 07 27 70
http://www.terranatura.com/inicio/index.aspxs

Terra Mitica is not the only noteworthy animal park in Costa Blanca, there is another that is just as interesting, but offers a singular experience that makes it distinctive among local theme parks. Terra Natura is a place that provides for its visitors the chance to immerse themselves in nature. It's not just a typical zoo experience, it's something involving much more.

Terra Natura is a wildlife park that gives its guests the chance to go on African Safari, right on the Mediterranean coast. It is an enclosure of 320,000 square meters, and an experiment in artificial habitat that feels just like the real thing. With 1500 animals and 200 different species, a quarter of those endangered, the sheer volume is overwhelming. And there's more in the park than just animals, Terra Natura is home to almost 200 species of trees, in addition to a number of other rare plant life.

Also, a trip to Terra Natura is as entertaining as it is educational. The park puts on a series of shows and adventure activities that make a visit here fun for the whole family. It's open to the public all year. For adults prices are set at €25, and for children its €20. Discount tickets are available for large groups as well.

Stroll the Explanada de España, Alicante

Located southwest of El Barrio, right alongside the harbor

Easily one of the most beautiful promenades in all of Spain, the Explanada de España sits alongside the harbor, offering a chance for visitors to stroll in view of the etherial Mediterranean Sea. The walkway is an ornately designed marble pathway lined on both sides by lush palm trees. Artists meticulously arranged 6.5 million floor tiles to create the magnificent wavy pattern in the promenade. It's one of the most romantic places in the city, as people come to take long walks in the glow of the sunset over the harbor. The pathway is accompanied by rows of storefronts, bistros, and fine dining restaurants. Frequently, musical event take place here, as it is a favorite gathering place among locals and visitors alike.

Eat Chocolate in Villajoyosa

Villajoyosa, Costa Blanca, Spain

In the luxurious province of Alicante adjacent to the revered ancient city of Valencia lies the hidden gem of Villajoyosa, Spain. The name of the town translates to mean "the joyful village," and has earned its name for a variety of reasons.

The charming streets lead to decadent beaches, encased by the sprawling richness of the majestic Mediterranean Sea. But more so than any of these stunning attributes, the town of Villajoyosa is famous for its chocolate.

Lying just south of Benidorm, the chocolate city of Villajoyosa offers a delectable experience that gives visitors the envied opportunity to bask in the sunlight and indulge in magnificent chocolate. The brand created here is called Valor, and it is a name revered throughout Europe for its sweet flavors and original style. Rumor has it that you can smell the atmospheric aroma of the chocolate before you even reach the city. The local specialty is chocolate with churros.

But, if chocolate is not your thing, Villajoyosa is also home to a variety of long beaches, fascinating history, and exciting water sports that you can't find anywhere else in Costa Blanca.

Bask in the Shade of Palms of Elche

Elche, Costa Blanca, Spain

An incredible excursion opportunity during your visit to Costa Blanca is a day trip to the luscious town of Elche. This city contains a unique history, and an even more singular distinction. It is known throughout Spain, and the international community, as being the world capital of palm trees. This unique characteristic has made a place for the Alicante city as a World Heritage site, established in 2001. The city is located just southwest of Alicante, and can be accessed by bus or car via highway N-30.

But Elche is more than just Palm Trees, it is also a thriving community with a rising economy, especially in the areas of shoe and clothing manufacturing and sweets. It has been a significant addition to Costa Blancan Society for hundreds of years. Elche is also home to the historic Basilica of Saint Mary, and each year a performance called "The Mystery of Elche" is reenacted, telling the story of the life of the Virgin Mary. Visitors from all over Spain come to Elche during this time, to watch the performance, and to reconnect with their religious heritage.

Recommendations for the Budget Traveller

Places to Stay

Accommodations in Costa Blanca include a variety of different styles, amenities, prices, and locations. Choosing a place to stay here has more to do with proximity than anything else, and avoiding the places which tend to be overcrowded. Costa Blanca is a city that invites tourists from all over the world to come and bask in the Mediterranean sun, so finding a hotel isn't always the easiest of choices. However, if you book early, you're not only sure to get great prices, but better views. Places to stay in Costa Blanca include tall skyscrapers and charming coastal villas. No matter what suits your fancy, there's something to fit your style in Costa Blanca.

Gran Hotel Bali, Benidorm

Calle del Actor Luis Prendes,
4 03502 Benidorm, Spain
+965 85 42 43
€80-€120

In the town of Benidorm lies the tallest hotel, at 186m, on the European continent.

The Gran Hotel Bali is an anthem to the rising development of Costa Blanca, inviting people from all over the world to visit and enjoy the stunning views of the surrounding areas from one of the highest rooms in the structure. The amenities of this hotel leave nothing to be desired either, with two restaurants, Turkish steam baths, and ornate balconies attached to rooms - you'll be staying at the door of luxury in this hotel in Benidorm, at affordable prices. And, the hotel is only a short walk from the famous beach, La Playa de Poniente.

Hotel Abaco Altea

C/ Salva 13, 03590 Altea, Spain
+011 34 966 88 25 00
http://www.abacoinnaltea.com/
€90-€122

If you are looking for a truly beautiful place to stay, away from the touristy mayhem in greater Costa Blanca, than the perfect hotel for you on your visit to the region is the radiant Hotel Abaco in Altea. Although slightly distant from the main attractions in the Alicante Province, this grand hotel is one of the most breathtaking accommodations in the area. The original Spanish architecture, the stunning Mediterranean views, and the picturesque setting combine to make a stay at Hotel Abaco one of the most inviting in all of Costa Blanca.

Servigroup Nereo, Benidorm

Avda L' Ametlla de Mar, 12, 03503
Benidorm, Spain
+965 85 07 07
http://www.servigroup.com/contenidos/hoteles/servigroup_nereo.html
€56-€125

Widely reviewed as one of the most inviting, friendly places to stay in the city of Benidorm, Servigroup Nereo is an affordable, easy choice for your visit to Costa Blanca. In a great part of the city, conveniently located to some of the most important attractions in Benidorm, this hotel offers superb amenities at affordable costs. The food is great, the staff is friendly, the atmosphere inviting, and the hotel is clean. Servigroup Nereo has everything that can make the duration of your stay in Costa Blanca a comfortable one.

Villa Del Mar Hotel, Benidorm

Avenida Armada Espanola, 03500
Benidorm, Spain
Telephone
hotelvilladelmar.com.es
€81-€286

One of the remarkable things about Villa Del Mar is that it's not the only one. This means that guests at the hotel are given a card which allows them to have discounts at similar hotels all over Spain, making it the best hotel to stay in if you plan to be in Costa Blanca for a while.

The staff is friendly, and the location is excellent as it is only a stone's throw from the Old Town of Benidorm. At Villa Del Mar you can lounge in comfort, eat at fabulous on site restaurants, or rest on a sun bed by the pool. It's an accommodation that is dedicating to ensuring that the guests have an incredible time, so much so that they will want to return someday.

Hospes Amerigo, Alicante

Rafael Altamira 7, 03002 Alicante, Spain
+011 34 914 36 34 78
€100-€180

This hotel in Alicante offers five star services at affordable prices. The rooms are exquisite, the location is excellent, and the staff is friendly. Situated in the center of Alicante, Hospes Amerigo is a short walk to the basic attractions of Alicante. It also possesses a rooftop terrace from which you can see the stunning layout of Alicante. Many rooms boast these views as well. Amenities include free wi-fi and breakfast, a full service health spa, and a number of onsite bars and restaurants.

Places to Eat & Drink

Alicante cuisine is a genre of food that is entirely its own. Although it has gleaned influences from its neighbors throughout the Mediterranean, the cuisine offered in Costa Blanca is unique, flavorful, and fresh. There is a premiere focus on the importance of rice and fish, with subtle Mediterranean flair. In addition to these staples, the culinary stylings of Alicante include a variety of locally grown fruits and vegetables - and don't forget the wine from local vineyards, especially rosés, reds, and clarets.

Déjà Vu, Benidorm

C/ Santa Faz 9
Benidorm 03501
Alicante, Spain
+965 859 693
http://www.dejavuspain.com/index.php/Find-Us/benidorm-restaurant.html
€8-€12

Situated in the charming Casco Antiguo, Old Town Benidorm, Déjà Vu is an intimate restaurant, seating only 24 people. The elegant inner décor offers a delightful ambiance, every detail is taken into account. You can order a 3 course meal for less than €9 that includes a glass of wine. The menu rotates with season, and contains local, savory fare that won't leave you unsatisfied.

Bocaito, Alicante

Isabel la Católica, 22
Muelle de Levante, 6
Alicante, Spain
+965922630
€20-€40

This tapas style authentic Spanish eatery in Alicante offers one of the best meals that you could have during your visit to Spain. The possessor of an esteemed Michelin star, Bocaito has a unique style that sets it apart from the standard fare of Costa Blanca. It accommodates guests that have a variety of tastes, and serves up delicious Mediterranean food that is memorable. And for a fine dining establishment, the prices are not unreasonable. Make your dining experience unforgettable with a meal at Bocaito.

Nou Manolin, Alicante

Calle de Villegas, 3, 03001 Alicante, Spain
+ 965 20 03 68
http://www.noumanolin.com/
€8-€25

One of the 101 best restaurants to eat at while in Europe, Nou Manolin is an excellent choice when looking for a great meal in Costa Blanca. The cuisine offered here is the apex of Alicante cuisine, serving delicious local dishes with the freshest of seasonal ingredients.

It is situated in the center of Alicante, and has become a culinary landmark for both natives and travelers. With excellent choices of wine, seafood, and authentic Spanish fare, you won't regret visiting Nou Manolin while in Costa Blanca.

Kataria Gastronomica, Benidorm

Av del Mediterráneo, 13
03503 Benidorm, Spain
+966 83 13 72
www.katariagastronomica.com/
€15-€30

Kataria Gastronomica is Mediterranean fine dining at its best. The atmosphere is sophisticated and subtly elegant. It is on the side of Benidorm that has adapted to contemporary trends, and as a result is on the cutting edge of culinary creativity. It's Alicante food with a twist, offering modern adaptation of classic Costa Blanca dishes. The restaurant has been widely reviewed for its remarkable attention to detail, especially in regards to presentation, and the quality of the food is there to back this up as well. It is one of the few true gourmet restaurants in Benidorm, and choosing to eat here is a delight that is unmatched throughout the whole of Costa Blanca.

El Chipiron Freiduria, Alicante

Zona Levante, s/n, módulo 1, local 1
03001 Alicante - Spain
+34(965)201174
€15-€30

This exquisite seafood restaurant showcases the decadence of Mediterranean cuisine. With incredible atmosphere, and delicious seafood, a meal at El Chipiron in Alicante is sure to be a great one. They serve remarkable fare, at reasonable prices, and maintain a level of quality that sets it amongst the best in Costa Blanca. If you're looking to have fantastic seafood without the unnecessary pretentiousness of standard gourmet restaurants, El Chipiron is certainly the place for you during your stay in Costa Blanca.

Places to Shop

Just like the rest of the characteristics of Costa Blanca, shopping is an experience that can vary from the height of modern class in a contemporary shopping mall to the quaint wanderings through antique flea markets and open plazas. Leather, jewelry, clothing, souvenirs - anything you can imagine - you can find on your trip to Costa Blanca. And, most likely, whatever you find is going to have a unique Spanish flair that isn't found anywhere else in the world.

Plaza Mayor at Casco Antiguo, Benidorm

In the old town of Benidorm sits the Plaza Mayor, a Mediterranean epicenter for food, shopping and entertainment. Casco Antiguo is one of the most charming points in the city to visit, because it contains one of Benidorm's last remaining vestige of old Spain. It is here that you're most likely to find original handcrafts, antiques, and irresistible souvenirs that you won't be able to live without. Shop in style at the Plaza Mayor in the old town of Benidorm, it's just as much of a cultural experience as it is a shopping trip; and while you're there, you're sure to find something that you'll absolutely love.

La Marina Shopping Center, Benidorm

La Marina Commercial Estate, Benidorm, Costa Blanca, Spain

True to form, Costa Blanca hosts a variety of shopping that is on the cutting edge of fashion and modern technology. One of the best places to do this is in the La Marina Shopping Center in the city of Benidorm. It is one of the largest shopping plazas in Spain and contains hundreds of stores sporting all kinds of goods. Anything from high-end labels, to toy shops, and electronics, La Marina is a one stop spot for your serious shopping needs while in Costa Blanca.

Guitarras Cashmira, Gata de Gorgos

Calle Estacion 25, Gata de Gorgos, Costa Blanca, Spain
+34 96 575 6320

Just outside of the city of Benidorm lies an exquisite destination that you shouldn't miss while on vacation in Costa Blanca. Even if you're not a musician, a trip to the Guitarras Cahmira in the town of Gata de Gorgos is a step into the history of Spanish culture, and an unforgettable experience of art and music. The store is steeped in history, and musical instruments displayed are examples of a tradition of music and woodwork that extends for centuries in Costa Blanca. Come and watch as artisans form guitars, designing them according to custom. It's a sight definitely worth seeing.

El Cisne Flea Market, Benidorm

N-332, Benidorm, Costa Blanca, Spain

In the trendy area of Centro, in Benidorm, you can find the fascinating weekend flea market El Cisne. It is an outdoor bargain market where natives and visitors join together to look for hidden gems. Anything you could possibly imagine can be found at this enormous market, and stalls extend farther than the eye can see. It is an unconventional shopping experience, with a setting more similar to a bazaar. Guests are expected to haggle - and odds are, you'll find amazing things at affordable prices. The market opens every Sunday, and once a month on Saturday as well.

Artesano de Polop, Benidorm

Plaza de los Chorros 3, Benidorm, Costa Blanca, Spain
+34 96 689 5704

Combining designer style with state of the art technology, Artesano de Polop is a creative shoe store located in the heart of Benidorm. Here you can find an array of quality, colorful shoes able to suit every style and taste. Fashion is popular in Costa Blanca, and the exciting variety of shoes available is an example of this. The region is also a specialist in hand made leather products, and this shoe store boasts a large amount of unique shoes that you wouldn't be able to find anywhere else.

Printed in Great Britain
by Amazon